PRAISE FOR
JAIMIE ENGLE

Kirkus Editor's Choice "Metal Mouth"
Amazon #1 New Release "Pets of Elsewhere"
L. Ron Hubbard Writers of the Future Award "The Dredge"
Publishers Book Life Prize in Fiction & Non-Fiction for
"Metal Mouth" and "Write a Book that Doesn't Suck"
Top 10 Kid Lit Reviews "Clifton Chase and the Arrow of Light"

"...the world Engle has created in (Dreadlands: Wolf Moon) is an intriguing one, equal parts familiar and fantastic." *Kirkus Reviews*

"...(Clifton Chase) belongs on your bookshelf - young or old - right along with Tolkien and Grimm." –*Amazon.com 5-star*

"I did not want to leave (The Dredge) until the last page was turned." –*Kid Lit Reviews*

"(Metal Mouth) presents troubled adolescence and romance through the eyes of a remarkable protagonist." –*Kirkus Editor's Choice*

"(Pets of Elsewhere) was fascinating, thrilling, and game me goosebumps both times." –*Amazon.com 5-star*

"Jaimie Engle brings "The Dredge" to an exciting, unexpected, and ultimately satisfying ending." –*Third Flatiron Editor*

BOOKS BY JAIMIE ENGLE

FICTION for kids

Clifton Chase and the Arrow of Light, Book 1
A boy time travels to rescue two princes

Clifton Chase on Castle Rock, Book 2
The adventure continues, only this time it's with Robin Hood

Clifton Chase and the Arrow of Light, Coloring Book
Condensed version of the novel with pictures to color

The Dredge
Supernatural gifts are sought through deception in a future world

Pets of Elsewhere, Book 1
Ghost animals haunt children in St. Augustine to tell their story

Dreadlands: Wolf Moon
A Viking boy must face shifting wolves or become their prey

Dreadlands: Blood Moon
Mayan bat god attacks the realm of Vithalia

The Toilet Papers, Jr.
Short story collection of humor, horror, & fairy tales

Metal Mouth
A girl's braces transmit a boy's voice after she's struck by lightning

FICTION for adults

The Toilet Papers: Places to Go, While you Go
Short story collection of humor, horror, and historical fiction

Just Jake (based off the movie)
A music superstar goes home and falls back in love with his sweetheart

Shell Game
A woman searches for her fiancé's killer in this 90s sleuth thriller

NON-FICTION

Clifton Chase and the Arrow of Light Teacher Guide
Teacher Curriculum Guide to use with the novel

Write a Book that Doesn't Suck (Lessons from the Engleverse #1)
A No-Nonsense Guide to Writing Epic Fiction

Write a Film that Doesn't Suck (Lessons from the Engleverse #2)
A No-Nonsense Guide to Writing Epic Film

How to Publish Your Book
A step-by-step ebook to get your book published

You Can Write a Comic Book
A book of panels and speech balloons to craft your own comic

Plotting Profits
Creating Diverse Income Streams from Your Stories

Plotting Profits

Creating Diverse Revenue Streams From Your Content

Jaimie Engle

Based off the presentation by Jaimie Engle, this
book is a work of non-fiction.

Text copyright © 2024 Jaimie Engle
Cover design © 2024 The Write Engle
The text for this book is set in Fairfield
All rights reserved, including the right of reproduction
in whole or in part in any form.

Published in the United States by The Write Engle, LLc

Visit us on the Web: www.JaimieEngle.com

Educators and librarians, for an author visit
or bulk order discounts, email Jaimie@JaimieEngle.com.

Summary: Creating Diverse Revenue Streams From Your Content

ISBN: 9798326837110
Imprint: Independently published

For my dad.

JAIMIE ENGLE
PLOTTING PROFITS

Create Diverse Revenue Streams
From Your Stories

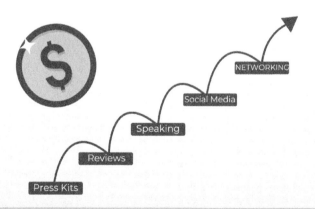

Introduction
Why This Book?

Welcome to the world of writing, where your imagination knows no bounds, and your words have the power to transport readers to far-off lands. My name is Jaimie Engle. I'm an award-winning hybrid novelist and a produced screenwriter. I've been writing since age seven, but published my first book in 2013. Since then, I've self-published (to date) twenty titles, with my film adaptation traditionally published through a small press.

In 2020, I added screenwriting to my resume and sold my first screenplay "Just Jake," which was produced and aired on network tv in 2023. It's been an insane journey and I've learned so many lessons along the way, many of which I arrived at after much trial and more error. Whether you're a seasoned wordsmith or just beginning your literary journey, one thing remains constant: the desire to share your stories with the world.

I know you want to evoke emotions, and spark endless possibilities with your books and scripts. But in today's ever-evolving landscape, being a successful writer entails more than just penning a captivating tale. It requires adaptability, innovation, and a willingness to explore unconventional paths to monetize your craft. You must learn to pivot on a dime to make a dollar. Gone are the days when simply publishing a book guaranteed financial stability. We live in a commoditized world with a low cost of entry. Many creators give away their product or service for free lowering the expectation and feasibility for writers to make a living wage.

Our connection to our books, our brands, are what enable us to write what we love and make a living. When I first published, the number to go full time was three books. When I published three, it had grown to ten, and today it's more than two dozen. Now, more than ever, authors must think outside the box, leveraging their creativity to build diverse revenue streams that extend beyond the pages of their manuscripts and scripts.

In my book, "Plotting Profits," we will embark on a journey together to unlock the secrets of turning your literary creations into sustainable sources of income. Whether you're a novelist, screenwriter, or non-fiction writer, the principles shared within these pages are designed to help you maximize your earning potential and thrive in today's competitive market.

We'll explore a myriad of avenues for generating revenue from your books, from traditional publishing to self-publishing, audiobooks to merchandise, speaking engagements to online courses and more to include adapting your book to film. Each chapter is packed with practical advice, real-life examples, and actionable strategies to empower you to take control of your writing career and turn your passion into profit.

So, grab your preferred writing instrument, settle into your favorite cozy corner, and let's begin this journey together. Your next chapter starts now!

One
Find Your Writer Band

In the vast world of writing, where creativity reigns supreme, it's essential to understand where you fit in the grand scheme of things. Just like in the music industry, where bands range from humble garage setups to global sensations, writers too can be categorized into different tiers based on their aspirations, achievements, and dedication to their craft. Each level requires different knowledge, investment, and time which produces equal parts reward, income, and status. The purpose of this example is to get you thinking about your place in the hierarchy for realistic expectations. Let's take a look at the four types.

The Garage Writers

Imagine the classic image of a group of friends jamming away in a garage, fueled by passion, dreams of stardom, and perhaps a few cans of soda. These are the Garage Writers of the literary world. They're the beginners, the enthusiasts, the ones who write because they love it, not necessarily because they expect fame or fortune to come knocking on their door (though they're not against it).

Garage Writers are characterized by their raw talent, unpolished skills, and boundless imagination. They may write for personal enjoyment, to express themselves, or simply to explore the wonders of storytelling. Their works might not always be polished gems, but they're brimming with potential and the sheer joy of creation. They may blog, write fan fiction, or share at poetry nights. We all start here.

A Garage Writer who queries their first manuscript faces rejection after rejection without reason. If they decide the agents and editors just don't "get them or their work" they may self-publish, or worse, pay a vanity press to self-publish for them. Don't get me wrong. I am not saying only amateurs self-publish. I am simply stating what I've seen, in my experience working with writers over the past decade. Many self-published books hit the market way too early in the editing process.

The problem arises when Garage Writers have unrealistic expectations. They've written a book, which means an agent should want to represent them or a publisher should want to publish them. If only it were that simple. Their distorted reality says they are officially professionals, even though they have not done the work to achieve that claim. They refuse to believe their book is not ready for the world. They publish before they have finished the final draft.

It takes years to achieve the ten thousand hours necessary to learn the craft of writing and how to execute a well-written story. It requires draft after draft of edits and large financial investments in yourself as a budding business. Garage Writers who do not wish to invest money in hiring a coach, working with a mentor, paying a professional editor, or taking classes to improve their craft, flood the marketplace with poor work. This makes it harder for consumers to find those high-quality books written by dedicated novelists.

A Garage Writer who wants to climb the ladder knows their books are not ready to be in the hands of readers, and are excited to invest in their writing careers. In contrast, a Garage Writer who accepts their place will continue to write and may even self-publish. The difference is they know their book is subpar and they are okay with that. Many writers have told me their books aren't perfect but they didn't have the patience required to keep editing, so they self-published without expectations of great sales or a huge following. That's a true Garage Writer!

The Local Writers

Moving up the ladder, we encounter the Local Writers, akin to the local bands that carve out a niche following in their communities. These writers have honed their craft to a certain extent, producing works that resonate with a specific audience or genre. They may have published a book or two, gaining recognition within their circles, but they haven't quite reached the pinnacle of literary success.

Local Writers are dedicated to their craft, investing time and effort into improving their skills and building their readership. While they may not achieve widespread fame or financial freedom, they find fulfillment in connecting with their audience and making a meaningful impact on a smaller scale. These writers can continue to improve their craft, network, and reach through speaking, teaching, and expanding into other fields beyond books. We will look at those options in the chapter on Cross Mediums.

When I first started publishing books, I realized I was spending time and money investing in social media ads to reach a global market. Then, one day in the grocery store, a little girl walked by and it hit me that she had no idea I was a writer. She had never read my books. Why was I spending resources trying to reach the world when the students at the 100+ schools in my county had not yet been reached? I decided then and there that I would become the biggest Local Writer in my county. From there, I would branch out into the state, an endeavor I am finally making traction in a decade later. Consider your local marketplace before you start trying to compete with the Pattersons and Rowlings of the world.

The Cover Writers

As we ascend further, we encounter the Cover Writers and the Professionals, equivalent to cover bands and touring musicians who make a living from their art. Cover Writers, or Ghostwriters, are like the musicians who play other people's songs, ghostwriting for a living. They may not always receive recognition for their work, but they excel in adapting their writing style to meet the demands of clients and markets.

On the other hand, the Professionals are the writers who have turned their passion into a full-fledged career. They've landed agents, signed book deals, and seen their works grace the shelves of bookstores. Writing is not just a hobby for them; it's their livelihood. They may not be household names, but they enjoy a steady income and the satisfaction of doing what they love for a living.

This is the goal of most writers in my circles. They just want to pay their bills with their art, whatever that looks like. I can imagine you are one of those writers or you wouldn't be investing your time in reading a book about making more money with your stories. This is a long road for every "overnight sensation." It is possible to find your pot of gold at the end of the literary rainbow, but you have to be willing to work your book business like a business. That means 40-hour work weeks, continuing education, constant networking, daily writing and rewriting, and learning the business side of websites, taxes, employees, and everything that goes into a successful entrepreneurial endeavor.

The Superstars

And then, there are the Superstars—the elite few who transcend their art to become cultural icons. These are the J.K. Rowlings and Stephen Kings of the writing world, whose names evoke awe and admiration wherever they go. Superstars are not made overnight; they're the result of talent, hard work, and perhaps a sprinkle of luck and timing.

Becoming a superstar writer is the dream of many, but it's not something that can be forced or rushed. In fact, it is one of those things that you can't actually set a goal to achieve. Superstars are made by the fans. So, you need to keep that in mind when you are writing your books, crafting your marketing, planning your speaking, and even down to the genre, age, and method of delivery of your stories. If you focus on becoming a superstar, then you miss the journey and all the wrungs on the ladder you must climb first. Instead, focus on becoming the best version of yourself as a writer, continuously honing your craft, and seizing opportunities when they arise. Who knows? With dedication, perseverance, and a stroke of serendipity, you might just pen that one book that propels you into literary superstardom.

Whether you're a Garage Writer strumming away in the shadows, a Local Writer making waves in your community, a Cover Writer earning a living through your words, a Professional Writer navigating the publishing world, or a dreamer aspiring to Superstardom, remember that each step of the journey is valuable. Embrace your role, embrace your voice, and never stop chasing your writing dreams. After all, every great band had to start somewhere—why should your writing journey be any different?

Challenge

Take an honest look at your writing abilities, financial situation, and time flexibility to assess your current wrung on the Writer Ladder. Each level up requires more ability, finances, and availability. I challenge you to evaluate where you are, where you want to be, and why. Finding satisfaction at whichever level you choose is what's important. Understanding the limitations and rewards of each "Band Type" requires honesty, introspection, and acceptance. There is no right or wrong level, just a right or wrong frame of mind regarding where you are and where you want to be. Once you can reconcile the two, you will find your perfect writing experience!

Two
The Heart of Your Journey

In the vast expanse of the literary landscape, where words are both the brushstrokes of imagination and the currency of communication, every writer embarks on a journey fueled by a deeper purpose—a reason that transcends the allure of fame and fortune, a guiding light that illuminates the path through the darkest valleys and the highest peaks.

Your "why" is the beating heart of your writer's journey, the North Star that guides you through the storms of rejection, the fog of self-doubt, and the wilderness of creative block. It is more than a mere aspiration for success; it is the essence of your literary legacy, the soulful resonance that echoes through every word you weave into existence.

Finding your "why" is about uncovering the core of your being, the passion that ignites your soul and compels you to pick up the pen or tap away at the keyboard, even when the odds seem insurmountable. It transcends the desire for external validation and monetary gain, anchoring you to a deeper sense of purpose that infuses your writing with meaning and significance.

Your "why" is your compass, your directive, your mission statement in the journey of storytelling. It is the energy behind every word, every character, every plot twist—a relentless pursuit of truth, beauty, and connection in a world hungry for authentic human experiences.

Crafting your writer's mission is an introspective process—a soul-searching quest to articulate the essence of your creative vision and the legacy you aspire to leave behind. It is about distilling your dreams and aspirations into a concise statement—a tagline that serves as a constant reminder of your purpose and passion, anchoring you in the turbulent sea of the writing life.

Your "why" must be bigger than the book, bigger than the writer, bigger than the dream. It is the cornerstone of your creative journey, the bedrock upon which you build your literary legacy. Whether your dreams materialize into New York Times bestsellers or blockbuster films, your "why" remains the steady heartbeat that sustains you through the highs and lows of the writer's odyssey.

When I published my first book, I had no "why" and floundered for the first year. Then, a still small voice whispered, "Bullying," and everything changed. I realized my book was birthed because of my son's school bully, was based on a historical family's bullying, and included a fictionalized bullying relationship that drove the main character toward his growth. With that new knowledge, I repackaged, rebranded, and reimagined my book's place in the world. I reached out to schools and built an anti-bullying presentation that used my characters and my book to teach empathy, the golden rule, and the power of words in life and literature. The heart of my book transformed my world into that of a speaker, and that changed everything!

So, take a moment to delve into the depths of your soul, to unearth the treasures hidden within your heart. Find your "why," embrace it, nurture it, and let it fuel your literary endeavors with unwavering purpose and passion. For in the end, it is not the destination that defines your journey, but the journey itself—the profound, transformative, and deeply fulfilling quest to share your unique voice with the world.

Three
Building Your Authorial Arsenal

A Multifaceted Approach to Success

Congratulations on delving deeper into your journey as a writer and entrepreneur! As you continue to navigate the ever-evolving landscape of the literary world, it's essential to equip yourself with a diverse array of tools and strategies to maximize your success and impact. In this chapter, we'll explore a comprehensive approach to building your authorial arsenal—a toolkit designed to empower you to thrive in today's competitive market.

What to Expect:

1. **The Power of Press Kits:** Learn how to craft compelling press kits that showcase your work in the best possible light, attract media attention, and amplify your reach.

2. **Garnishing Reviews:** Discover the art of soliciting and leveraging book / movie reviews to build credibility, boost visibility, and connect with readers / viewers.
3. **Introduction to Selling Tools:** Explore essential selling tools and platforms that can help you expand your distribution channels, increase sales, and diversify your revenue streams.
4. **Utilizing Social Media:** Harness the power of social media to engage with your audience, cultivate a vibrant community of readers, and amplify your brand presence online.
5. **The Power of Your Website and Newsletter:** Learn how to optimize your website and newsletter as powerful marketing tools to drive traffic, nurture relationships with readers, and promote your content effectively.
6. **Integrating Speaking Engagements for Revenue:** Discover how speaking engagements can serve as lucrative opportunities to share your expertise, connect with audiences, and generate additional income streams.
7. **Best Practices for Self-Promotion:** Explore proven strategies and tactics for effectively promoting yourself and your work without feeling salesy or inauthentic.
8. **Building Your Content in Multiple Mediums:** Embrace the versatility of multimedia content creation to reach diverse audiences, enhance reader or viewer

engagement, and expand your brand across various platforms.

By mastering these essential components of the authorial arsenal, you'll be better equipped to navigate the intricacies of the modern publishing and screenwriting landscape, connect with readers or producers on a deeper level, and ultimately, achieve sustainable success as a writer and entrepreneur. So, let's dive in and start building the foundation for your continued growth and prosperity!

Four
The Power of Press Kits
Unlocking Your Media Potential

Press kits are indispensable tools for authors and filmmakers, serving as comprehensive packages that provide journalists, bloggers, and influencers with all the essential information they need to promote your work. By understanding the nuances of press kits and their components, you can effectively capture media attention and maximize your reach. This chapter will guide you through the process of creating impactful press kits, highlighting the differences between media releases and expert releases, and detailing each element that makes up a successful press kit.

Media Releases vs. Expert Releases

Media releases are announcements sent to the press to inform them of newsworthy events, such as a new book release, a film premiere, or a significant milestone. They are time-sensitive and focus on generating immediate media coverage.

In contrast, expert releases are evergreen bios and loglines sent to journalists to position yourself as an expert in your field. These releases are kept on file and used when journalists need an authoritative voice for a story. They highlight your expertise, background, and unique insights, establishing you as a go-to resource.

After speaking to the legislative committee about film funding in Florida, I have been contacted several times by journalists to discuss this topic, to include in-home interviews and news stories. As the resident "Florida film expert" I have established myself as a valuable resource while also building trust and relationships with various members of the press.

Activity:

Take a moment to jot down your areas of expertise. What subjects are you passionate about? Where do you have unique knowledge or experience? Use these to craft your expert releases.

Elements of a Press Kit

Press kits are my bread and butter. Every time I have an event, a new book, or a new film deal, I send a release to my growing contact base. It always results in a publication somewhere. It could be in print, on a website, or via the television studio, and every new moment of publicity brings more eyeballs to me and my work.

Here is a breakdown of what a typical press kit includes:

1. **Media Release Basics**
   - **FOR IMMEDIATE RELEASE:** This phrase should be at the top, indicating the information is ready for publication.
   - **Contact Information:** Include your name, email, and phone number.
   - **Header One:** A catchy headline to grab attention.
   - **Header Two:** Additional details to support the headline.
   - **Location and Date:** The origin of the release and the date it was issued.
   - **Opening Quote:** A statement from you or someone involved to add depth and perspective.
   - **First Paragraph:** The 5 W's (who, what, where, when, and why). This should provide a complete overview so a journalist can get the gist in one glance. It is single spaced without an indent.
   - **Subsequent Paragraphs:** Expand on the event and provide more context about you and your work. These subsequent paragraphs have a single space between.

- **Additional Quotes**: Include two to three quotes from you, event managers, or others involved. Be sure to place a space between each quote and each subsequent paragraph.
- **Call to Action (CTA)**: Encourage readers to take the next step, such as visiting your website, purchasing your book, or attending your event. Mention that headshots and additional photographs are available upon request. Include three hashtags at the end to let the journalist know you have reached the end of your release, with your bio to follow.

2. **Headshots:**
   - **Types to Include**: Professional, high-resolution images that reflect your personality and professionalism. Avoid casual or poorly lit photos.
   - **Attributes**: Always credit the photographer and provide links to your social media and website.

3. **Biography:**
   - **Different Lengths**: Prepare bios of various lengths for different purposes:
     - **Short Bio**: 50-100 words for quick introductions.
     - **Medium Bio**: 150-200 words for speaking engagements or event programs.

- **Long Bio**: 300-500 words for detailed profiles or interviews.
- **Topics Covered**: Tailor each bio to highlight relevant achievements, experience, and personal anecdotes that align with the context of its use

4. Book Metadata or Movie Info:
   - **Book Metadata**: Include the book title, subtitle, ISBN, publisher, publication date, genre, and a brief synopsis.
   - **Movie Info**: Include the film title, director, producers, main cast, release date, genre, and a brief synopsis.

Creating a Media Release: A Step-by-Step Breakdown

I reuse this template for every media release I send out. I also take advantage of the document by double dipping and posting it on my blog. It allows more exposure for my release on my website and connected social media sites. Here's what your release should look like:

1. FOR IMMEDIATE RELEASE
2. Contact Information

Your Name
Email
Phone Number

3. **Header One:**
An Engaging Headline
4. **Header Two:**
Supporting Information
5. **Location and Date:**
City, State - Month Day, Year
6. **Opening Quote:**
"A compelling quote from the author or relevant person to provide insight and context."
7. **First Paragraph:**
Include all the 5 W's (who, what, where, when, and why) succinctly.
8. **Subsequent Paragraphs:**
Expand on the event, providing more detailed information about the book or film, and your background.
9. **Additional Quotes:**
"Another insightful quote from the author or someone involved."
"A third quote to add depth and perspective."
10. **Call to Action**
Encourage the reader to visit your website, buy your book, or attend your event. Mention that high-resolution headshots and additional photographs are available upon request.

Reminder:

Always ensure that your media release provides everything a journalist needs to write the article without having to contact you for more information.

This efficiency increases the likelihood of your story being picked up. And having the option of "photos available upon request" or "Advanced copies available upon request" is good information to include in your email.

By mastering the elements of press kits and understanding the strategic differences between media and expert releases, you can significantly enhance your media outreach efforts. A well-prepared press kit not only positions you as a professional but also makes it easier for journalists to feature your work, ultimately expanding your reach and impact.

Media Release Example

The example below is a media release for my first movie and the novelization. It can be found on my website blog here: https://jaimieengle.com/2022/12/13/local-florida-writer-breaks-into-hollywood/

* * *

LOCAL FLORIDA WRITER BREAKS INTO HOLLYWOOD

Jaimie Engle Secures Film Production and Novelization for "Just Jake:

Satellite Beach, Florida, December 13th, 2022 – "The ones who make it, never give up!"

After ten years navigating the world of independent publishing, local writer Jaimie Engle took a huge risk with a monster payoff. In 2021, she officially paused her publishing house, geared toward upper elementary and middle grade books, to pursue a career in screenwriting, a profession comprised less than 30% by women. She wrote and sold her first feature film, *Just Jake*, a holiday romantic comedy in June 2022 to True Brand Entertainment's Executive Producer Brian Bird. The film, shot in Colorado Springs, CO, will release on UpTV Faith & Family Network and Super Chanel Heart & Home in 2023.

"When I was a little girl, I recorded *The Wizard of Oz* and wrote down all the dialogue," shared Engle, who began writing short stories in third grade. "At the time, I was fascinated with films, watching the same ones on repeat, with a dream to work in the movie business someday. I never thought I would see that dream come true!"

Just Jake is an uplifting story about a country music singer (played by Rob Mayes) who returns home after major writer's block, falls back in love with his high school sweetheart (played by Brittany Bristow), and together they rediscover love by making music. The film is directed by Brandon Clark.

Engle sold the book rights to Vinspire Publishing and completed the novelization for a publication release on August 29th, 2023. The book follows the storyline in Engle's original script and can be added to reader's Goodreads shelves prior to launch at https://bit.ly/JustJakeShelf.

"Once the script is purchased, it's out of my hands as far as the final product," shared Engle, regarding the novelization. "It was important for me to tell my story, so keeping the book rights and selling those allowed me to stay true to my version. After filming starts, the story always changes. Financial restrictions, sets, actors, and many other stipulations go into the actual production that don't exist in the writer's imagination. I'm the architect, but the filmmakers are the builders and artisans that bring the story to life."

Since writing *Just Jake*, Engle has completed 6 feature films and 3 television shows, which have all been optioned and are in various stages of development and pre-production. She speaks at conventions and schools on writing in film, books, television, and comics, weaving practical advice with experience.

"I love inspiring other people to reach for their dreams," shared Engle, who spent the past ten years speaking to students about social issues and the power of words. "My books are steppingstones to reach kids and discuss social issues like bullying, self-esteem, and voice, both in life and literature. I also love speaking to writers of all levels at conventions and conferences, in person and virtually. Lots of people have given me tools along the way and believed in me. It's a great feeling and honor to give that back."

To learn more about Jaimie Engle, her programs, books, and current film offerings, visit www.JaimieEngle.com or jaimie@jaimieengle.com.

BIO: Jaimie Engle writes stories with a magic touch for film, television, books, and comics. Her feature film JUST JAKE was sold to TrueBrand Entertainment for a streaming release on UpTV Faith & Family Network, and the novelization to Vinspire Publishing. Besides writing, Jaimie supports her sons in professional theater and varsity football with her husband in Florida. Fun fact? Jaimie danced at the halftime show of the Aloha Bowl in 1990. Follow the journey on social @JaimieEngleWrites.

Expert Release Example

My expert release on my website is a pdf that journalists can download, along with photographs and movie posters. You can check it out at www.JaimieEngle.com/press and see the example here:

EXPERT RELEASE

Email: jaimie@jaimieengle.com
Website: www.JaimieEngle.com
Social Media: @JaimieEngleWrites

When you think of overcoming adversity and making dreams come true, think of Jaimie Engle.

After her publisher disappeared a month before release date, Jaimie Engle was forced to launch her first novel on her own. She has faced an upward battle in publishing with incredible victories along the way to include prestigious awards, brick and mortar book signings, and sharing the stage with some of the industry's biggest names in children's books.

In 2021, Jaimie switched gears to writing for film and television. She wrote 8 feature films, 3 tv shows, 3 books, and a limited comic book series in one year, won numerous industry awards, and has her work in consideration with dozens of producers, major networks, and in production. Jaimie inspires through personal experience.

Book Jaimie Engle, award-winning writer and national speaker to discuss…

- Her inspiring story from book to screen to encourage others to never give up
- All aspects of writing techniques for books, screenplays, and comics
- Branding, marketing and positioning yourself in the digital world
- Overcoming adversity through agents, publishers, and indie publishing

Jaimie Engle Guest Expert Interview Credentials

- Active speaker on writing books and films/teleplays.
- Published author of 15 books and dozens of articles with 3 Amazon #1 New
Releases and 8 titles in the Amazon Top 100 Lists
- Produced screenwriter, multiple optioned screenwriter
- Recipient of the Kirkus Editor's Choice, Publisher's Marketplace Book Life
Prize in Fiction, and L. Ron Hubbard Writers of the Future Award
- Publisher's Marketplace Quarterfinalist in Book Life Prize for Non-Fiction
- Finalist in Austin Film Festival, Screencraft Contests, and Coverfly Contests

Publications:

Clifton Chase and the Arrow of Light, Clifton Chase on Castle Rock, Pets of Elsewhere, Dreadlands: Wolf Moon, Dreadlands: Blood Moon, Metal Mouth, The Dredge, The Toilet Papers, The Toilet Papers, Jr., Write a Book that Doesn't Suck, Write a Film that Doesn't Suck, How to Publish Your Book, Just Jake and more on the website under the books tab or wherever books are sold! Legal Representation: Darin Chavez, Tricarico Chavez, LLP

###

Next Steps

Once you have completed your media release, you will want to build out a list of local journalists in radio, print, and television. Create a spreadsheet so you can keep track of your list and update it each time you send out a release. You can also build out lists of bloggers, reviewers, podcasters, and YouTubers and let them know you are available to speak via your media release or your expert release.

I have lists for romance bloggers, podcasters, and reviewers, as well as comic book bloggers, podcasters, and reviewers. I have lists of local press in my county and the three surrounding counties, the state, and the country. You can build these lists out or you can pay for them. It's up to you. I recommend a service for emailing, like MailChimp, Constant Contact, or your website, which we will discuss in a later chapter.

Five
The Power of Reviews
Finding, Utilizing, and Maximizing Your Reviews

Book and movie reviews are invaluable assets in any writer's toolkit. They provide social proof, enhance credibility, and significantly influence potential readers' and viewers' purchasing decisions. In this chapter, we will explore the importance of reviews, where to find them, and how to use them to your advantage. We'll cover everything from pre-release reviews to leveraging social media platforms and reaching out to podcasters and YouTubers. Let's dive in and discover how to harness the power of reviews to boost your project's success.

The Importance of Book Reviews

One of the hardest and most valuable items in your author arsenal are book reviews. I have paid for them, offered free books, begged and stolen for them, and remind my followers every month in my newsletter to please review my books and films because it helps increase visibility for others to find my work. Most of the time, my pleading goes unanswered. Every now and then, I am gifted with a review.

My advice is to never give up and always ask. More than 100 views signifies that your story has reached beyond your circle of influence and makes the reviews unbiased. This should be your target number for every book and movie you write.

Book reviews serve multiple purposes:

> 1. **Credibility and Social Proof:** Positive reviews from reputable sources and readers help build trust and credibility with potential buyers.
> 2. **Increased Visibility:** Reviews can boost your book's visibility on platforms like Amazon and Goodreads, improving your chances of reaching a wider audience.
> 3. **Engagement:** Engaging with readers and viewers who review your book or film helps build a loyal community and encourages word-of-mouth marketing.

Where to Find Book Reviews

This is not an exhaustive list by any stretch of the imagination. With a simple web search, you can start with my list and build your own according to audience, genre, and budget.

1. **Major Review Sites:**
   - **Kirkus Reviews:** Known for their thorough and respected reviews. You can submit your book for a professional review.
   - **Northwest Review:** Another respected source that can provide credible and influential reviews.
   - **Publishers Weekly:** Offers reviews that are highly regarded in the publishing industry.
2. **Pre-Release Reviews:**
   - **NetGalley:** A platform where authors can offer digital ARCs (Advance Reader Copies) to a community of reviewers, librarians, and booksellers.
   - **Sprout:** A service that helps distribute ARCs and collects reviews before the official release.
   - **Goodreads:** You can find reviewers and groups or pay for a giveaway. More in a later chapter on Goodreads specifically.
3. **ARC Packages:**
   - **Metadata:** Include title, author, publication date, ISBN, genre, and a brief synopsis.

- **Review Instructions:** Provide clear instructions on how to submit reviews, including deadlines and preferred platforms.
- **Google Form:** Create a Google Form to collect names and contact information, which will help you build a CRM (Customer Relationship Management) list.

4. **Reader Review Platforms:**
   - **Amazon:** Encourage readers to leave reviews on Amazon, as they heavily influence purchasing decisions. You can search for a list of their best book reviewers and solicit them directly. Your Author page can be followed by fans.
   - **Goodreads:** A social platform for book lovers where reviews can increase your book's visibility and reader engagement.
   - **BookBub:** Known for its book discovery and recommendation features, reviews here can significantly impact your book's reach. Your author page can be followed by fans.
   - **BookSiren:** Although this is a paid site, it's awesome. For a small fee you upload your manuscript and only pay for downloads the site provides, guaranteed at 75%. Plus, you can set a cap on spending, choose review sites, and build

a following. They also allow you to share your link without paying for the downloads of your list. Your ARC package is created onsite for ease of sharing.

My Experience

I paid for a Kirkus Review for my novel *Dreadlands: Wolf Moon*. I didn't know it was through their "self-published" side. In my opinion, it wasn't worth the money because the audience of librarians and educators aren't looking for self-published books to stock their shelves. On the flip side, I bought ad space for my book *Metal Mouth* which gave it a good amount of visibility and it was selected as a Kirkus Editor's Choice Book (2020) awarded to around 2% of its books. It also received a Publisher's Weekly Book Life Prize in Fiction (2020).

On the non-fiction end, "Write a Book that Doesn't Suck" was honored with a Publisher's Weekly Book Life Prize in Non-Fiction (2020). I definitely advise submitting for the Publisher's Weekly Book Life Prize.

Leveraging Social Media for Reviews

In a subsequent chapter, we will delve into the importance of utilizing social media to engage with your audience and promote your work. Here we will take a look at ways to find reviewers on social.

1. **BookTok (TikTok)**: Reach out to influencers who review books and create engaging content to attract their audience.
2. **Bookstagram (Instagram)**: Engage with the Bookstagram community by sharing aesthetically pleasing photos of your book and connecting with book reviewers.
3. **BookTube (YouTube)**: Connect with BookTubers who review books and discuss literature, offering them ARCs for honest reviews and requesting interviews.

Approaching Podcasters and YouTubers

Podcasts and YouTube channels dedicated to books and literature are excellent platforms for reviews and interviews. Research relevant podcasters and YouTubers, and send them personalized messages along with your ARC package, highlighting why your book would interest their audience. Be prepared to send out physical copies, so make sure you aren't hitting up people in England if you're not willing to pay the shipping.

Expanding Your CRM List

Your list is YOURS! What I mean is you control the access you have to the people on your lists. Always add to and find ways to build your CRM. It is your secret sauce, your pot of gold, and your lifeblood as a writer. Here's how to work it:

1. **Journalists and Media Contacts:** Include book reviewers, podcasters, news reporters, and radio and TV personalities in your CRM list. Submit ARC packages and request reviews and interviews. Be prepared to send paperbacks and ebooks.
2. **Newsletter Subscribers:** Build your CRM list further through your newsletter subscribers, a topic we'll explore in detail in a later chapter.

Utilizing Book Reviews Effectively

One of the tricks I use with my ARC reviewers is asking for their review upon completion of the book, even before it's available for purchase. Then, when the book goes live, I send them back their review, with a link to the book on Amazon, Goodreads, and BookBub, and ask them to please copy and paste it on those three sites and their social media accounts with a link to Amazon. The reason I do this is because people forget and people are lazy. I know my readers WANT to help me out, so I WANT to make it as easy as possible for them to do so. After all, it benefits me and not them to get theirs reviews live and on site.

Another trick is utilizing the review in your pre-marketing campaigns. If you already have opinions of readers before you launch, it makes it much easier to promote the book with a third-party opinion. Whether it's before your launch or after, here's some next steps:

1. **Quotes for Marketing:** Use positive review quotes in your marketing materials, including your website, social media, and book cover.
2. **Engage with Reviewers:** Respond to reviews, thanking readers for their feedback and engaging in discussions to build a loyal community.
3. **Address Negative Reviews Professionally:** Handle negative reviews with grace and professionalism, using them as an opportunity to learn and improve. NEVER reply to a bad review. It makes you look BAD! Just move on and make more books.

The Importance of Movie Reviews

Just like book reviews, movie reviews play a crucial role in the success of a film. They provide social proof, enhance credibility, and can significantly influence potential viewers' decisions. Whether your film is an independent project or a major studio release, positive reviews can make a substantial difference in its reception and popularity.

Where to Find Movie Reviews

In much of the same way as book reviews, you can do a web search to find and build your own CRM. Here's a few of the top spots to get you started:

1. **Major Review Sites and Publications:**
    - **Rotten Tomatoes:** Aggregates reviews from critics and audiences, providing an overall score that is widely referenced.
    - **Metacritic:** Similar to Rotten Tomatoes, it aggregates reviews and assigns a weighted average score.
    - **IMDb:** Offers user reviews and ratings, as well as reviews from professional critics.
    - **The Hollywood Reporter:** A respected source for industry news and reviews.
    - **Variety:** Another top publication that provides detailed reviews and industry insights.
    - **RogerEbert.com:** Continuing the legacy of the famed critic, this site offers in-depth reviews from a variety of critics.
2. **Independent Reviewers and Blogs:**
    - **Film Threat:** Focuses on independent films, providing reviews and coverage that might not get mainstream attention.

- **IndieWire:** Offers reviews and news about independent films and filmmakers.
- **Slashfilm:** Covers a wide range of movies with a strong emphasis on independent and genre films.

3. **Pre-Release Reviews:**
   - **Film Festivals:** Submitting your film to festivals like Sundance, Tribeca, or SXSW can generate early reviews from critics and audiences.
   - **Screeners:** Sending out screeners to select critics and influencers can help build buzz before the official release.

4. **Audience Reviews:**
   - **Social Media:** Platforms like X, Facebook, and Instagram are great for gathering and showcasing audience reviews.
   - **Review Aggregator Sites:** Encourage audiences to leave reviews on sites like Rotten Tomatoes, IMDb, Amazon, and Metacritic.

How to Use Movie Reviews Effectively

Much like books, it's next to impossible to get reviews. As a note, whether it's a book or a film that you have enjoyed, take three minutes to share your thoughts via Amazon, your social media, or any of the other spots mentioned in this chapter. It helps the creators gain visibility and it's good karma. Pay it forward because the laws of sowing and reaping are real!

Once you have these gold nuggets of movie reviews or reviews of your screenplay via contest wins or paid coverage, here's how you can use them to your benefit:

1. **Marketing Materials:**
   - **Quotes for Promotions:** Use positive quotes from reviews in trailers, posters, and other promotional materials to attract potential viewers.
   - **Star Ratings:** Display star ratings prominently in your marketing efforts to quickly convey the film's reception.
2. **Social Media:**
   - **Share Reviews:** Regularly share positive reviews on your social media channels to engage with your audience and build credibility.
   - **Engage with Reviewers:** Thank reviewers and engage with their content to build relationships and encourage more coverage.
3. **Press Releases:**
   - **Highlight Positive Reviews:** Include excerpts from reviews in your press releases to capture media attention and lend authority to your film.

- **Create Buzz:** Use reviews to create buzz around your film, especially leading up to its release.
4. **Website:**
    - **Review Section:** Dedicate a section of your film's website to showcase reviews, ratings, and testimonials.
    - **Links to Full Reviews:** Provide links to full reviews for viewers who want to read more.

Conclusion

Both book and movie reviews are powerful tools that can significantly influence the success of your creative works. By understanding where to find these reviews and how to effectively use them, you can build credibility, increase visibility, and engage with your audience in meaningful ways. By strategically seeking reviews from reputable sources, leveraging social media platforms, and expanding your CRM list, you can maximize the impact of your book and movie reviews.

In the next chapter, I'll discuss book and film awards, which go hand-in-hand with reviews.

Six
The Power of Awards
Boosting Credibility and Visibility

Submitting your book and screenplay for awards is an excellent strategy to enhance your credibility, gain recognition, and increase your story's visibility. Winning or even being shortlisted for an award can significantly impact your book's or scripts' success and your reputation as a writer. It can help you connect with a reputable producer, director, agent, or manager.

In this chapter, we'll explore the importance of book and script awards, identify reputable awards, guide you on how to build a submission list, and show you how to use awards in your marketing efforts.

The Importance of Book Awards

Even if people don't "know" the award, I guarantee they are impressed when you can tell them your book is award-winning! In fact, besides the actual legitimate awards I've been honored to receive, I have also gained some pretty cool accolades like "Top 10 List" on Amazon. Sounds impressive, right? Well, would you still think so if I told you it was in the children's books / animals / wolves category for the release of my werewolf / Vikings young adult novel *Dreadlands: Wolf Moon*? It's called marketing and it's why you're reading this book.

The truth is that if you've written well, edited long, and produced a great product, whether on your own, with a small press or a big five publisher, awards are impressive. Having prestigious awards and some you've gathered through strategic tag words and submissions, will have a momentous impact on your book impressing a new buyer to say yes and give your writing a shot.

Here's why:

1. **Credibility and Prestige**: Winning or being nominated for a book award adds a layer of credibility and prestige to your work, making it more attractive to readers, publishers, and media.
2. **Increased Visibility**: Awards can generate media coverage and attract attention from new readers and industry professionals.
3. **Networking Opportunities**: Award ceremonies and events provide opportunities to network with other authors, publishers, and influencers in the literary world.

Identifying Legitimate Book Awards

This is key! While I am a big believer in all awards holding importance, I equally know you need to be smart with your dollars when you are entering awards competitions. Spending money on an award that doesn't mean much or spending it on one that has name recognition among readers or critics is a serious consideration.

Also, with so many places offering awards, you need to be extra careful you aren't funding someone's bank account without any benefit to your business. You can check out the following and build your list from here:

1. **Major Literary Awards:**
    - **Pulitzer Prize:** One of the most prestigious awards in literature, recognizing excellence in fiction, nonfiction, and poetry.
    - **National Book Award:** Celebrates outstanding literary work by American authors.
    - **Man Booker Prize:** Recognizes the best original novel written in English and published in the UK.
2. **Genre-Specific Awards:**
    - **Hugo Award:** Honors the best in science fiction and fantasy.
    - **Edgar Award:** Recognizes excellence in mystery writing.

- Romance Writers of America (RITA) Award: Celebrates outstanding romance novels and novellas.
- Caldecott Medal: Awarded annually to the artist of the most distinguished American picture book for children.

3. Independent and Self-Published Book Awards:
    - Kirkus Reviews: Offers a highly respected award for self-published and traditionally published books.
    - Publisher's Weekly BookLife Prize in Fiction and Non-Fiction: A competition that provides significant exposure to self-published authors.
    - Independent Publisher Book Awards (IPPY): Honors independent authors and publishers.
    - Next Generation Indie Book Awards: Recognizes and honors indie authors and independent publishers.
    - Writer's Digest Self-Published Book Awards: Celebrates the best self-published books.

4. Reader's Choice Awards:
    - Goodreads Choice Awards: Readers vote for their favorite books in various categories, giving winners significant visibility and credibility.

- **LibraryReads:** A monthly list of favorite new books recommended by library staff across the U.S.
5. **Regional and Niche Awards:**
    - **Foreword INDIES Book of the Year Awards:** Recognizes books from independent and university presses.
    - **Royal Palm Literary Awards:** Awarded by the Florida Writers Association.
    - **State Book Lists:** Many states have their own book awards and lists, such as the California Book Awards or the Texas Bluebonnet Award.

Building a Submission List

1. **Research Awards:** Start by researching awards relevant to your book's genre, format, and publication date. Use websites like Poets & Writers, Writer's Digest, and literary magazines that list book awards.
2. **Create a Spreadsheet:** Organize your findings into a spreadsheet with columns for award name, submission deadlines, eligibility criteria, entry fees, and contact information.
3. **Check Eligibility:** Ensure your book meets the eligibility criteria for each award before submitting.
4. **Prepare Submission Materials:** Gather the necessary materials for submission, which may

include copies of your book, author bio, synopsis, and entry fees.

Screenwriting Awards

In addition to the importance of book awards, screenplay awards and competitions are crucial for writers looking to gain recognition, credibility, and opportunities in the film and television industry. Winning or placing in these competitions can open doors to agents, producers, and studios. Here are some reputable screenplay awards and competitions to consider:

1. The Black List:

- **Overview:** An annual survey of the most liked unproduced screenplays in Hollywood.
- **Benefits:** Scripts that make The Black List gain significant industry attention and often lead to production deals and representation.

2. Stage 32:

- **Overview:** A platform that offers various screenplay competitions throughout the year, including feature films, TV pilots, and shorts.
- **Benefits:** Winners often receive meetings with industry professionals, script consultations, and membership benefits on Stage 32.

3. Coverfly:

- **Overview:** A hub for various screenplay competitions, with a comprehensive database of contests and fellowships.
- **Benefits:** High-ranking scripts on Coverfly's The Red List gain exposure to industry professionals, and the platform provides feedback and tracking tools for writers.

4. Final Draft Big Break Contest:

- **Overview:** An annual competition hosted by Final Draft, one of the leading screenwriting software companies.
- **Benefits:** Winners receive cash prizes, software, and industry meetings, along with significant exposure.

5. Nicholl Fellowships in Screenwriting:

- **Overview:** A prestigious competition run by the Academy of Motion Picture Arts and Sciences.
- **Benefits:** Winners receive substantial cash awards and the opportunity to meet and be mentored by industry veterans.

6. Austin Film Festival Screenplay Competition:

- **Overview:** One of the most respected competitions, known for helping writers break into the industry.

- **Benefits:** Winners and finalists are invited to the festival, where they can network with filmmakers, producers, and agents.

7. **Sundance Screenwriters Lab:**

    - **Overview:** A prestigious program that selects a handful of writers to develop their scripts with the support of established professionals.
    - **Benefits:** Participants receive mentorship, workshops, and networking opportunities at the Sundance Film Festival.

8. **PAGE International Screenwriting Awards:**

    - **Overview:** A worldwide competition that recognizes excellence in screenwriting across multiple genres.
    - **Benefits:** Winners receive cash prizes, software, and marketing support to promote their scripts to the industry.

9. **BlueCat Screenplay Competition:**

    - **Overview:** A competition that offers detailed feedback to all entrants, with categories for features, shorts, and pilots.
    - **Benefits:** Winners receive cash prizes, software, and exposure to industry professionals.

10. **Script Pipeline:**

- **Overview**: A competition that seeks to discover up-and-coming screenwriters and connect them with industry opportunities.
- **Benefits**: Winners receive cash prizes, script development assistance, and introductions to industry contacts.

I submitted a tv pilot to Austin Film Festival in 2022. It did not place. I worked with a mentor, made changes, and resubmitted the following year and I was honored as a "Second Rounder" with a personal phone call from an AFF rep to tell me I had placed in their contest. It was pretty awesome and showed me my work had improved. It's a legitimate accolade that impresses the right people in the industry.

Submitting your screenplay to reputable awards and competitions is a strategic way to gain recognition, build credibility, and open doors to new opportunities in the film and television industry. Just as with book awards, doing well in these contests can significantly boost your visibility and career prospects. Use the insights and benefits of these competitions to plan your submissions and increase your chances of success.

Using Awards in Your Marketing

1. **Website and Social Media**: Display award badges, announcements, and logos on your website and social media profiles to highlight your achievements.

2. **Press Releases:** Issue press releases to announce your award wins or nominations, and share the news with your media contacts.
3. **Book Cover and Promotional Materials:** Include award logos and mentions on your book cover, in your author bio, and in promotional materials to enhance your book's appeal.
4. **Script One Sheet:** Add the laurels to your one sheets and share on social.
5. **Newsletter:** Share your award news with your newsletter subscribers to keep them engaged and informed about your successes.

A Unique Celebration: Jolabokaflod

One of the most enchanting literary traditions is Jolabokaflod, or the "Christmas Book Flood," in Iceland. This delightful custom involves giving books as gifts on Christmas Eve and spending the night reading. Jolabokaflod is a testament to the power of books to bring people together and create cherished memories.

Authors can draw inspiration from this tradition to promote their books during the holiday season, encouraging readers to embrace the joy of giving and reading books. By incorporating the spirit of Jolabokaflod into your marketing strategy, you can create unique campaigns that resonate with book lovers and celebrate the magic of reading.

Conclusion

Submitting your book and screenplays for awards is a strategic way to build credibility, increase visibility, and enhance your reputation as a writer. By identifying legitimate awards, building a submission list, and effectively using awards in your marketing, you can maximize the impact of these accolades on your book's and script's success.

Seven
Selling Tools
Turning Creativity into Commerce

As writers and creatives, it's natural to focus on the art of storytelling and leave the selling to someone else. However, in today's commodity-driven market, mastering the art of selling is essential for success. This chapter explores various selling tools that can help you market your books and scripts effectively. From creating engaging trailers to running book giveaways, we'll cover a range of strategies to turn your creativity into commerce.

Book and Movie Trailers

Engaging customers and promoting your work can be a full-time job. Whether you're going it alone, have an assistant, or a team working with you, you are a business owner who needs to market and promote your products and services. For video options, you can always use your smart phone to film, edit, and upload to YouTube. For a little more "oomph" try this:

1. **DIY Trailers**: Tools like Canva and Bookbrush allow you to create your own book and movie trailers using stock footage and customizable templates. Ensure that any footage or music used is cleared for commercial use. This isn't my area of expertise, so I recommend a good web search for more options.
2. **Hiring Professionals**: If your budget allows, consider hiring a videographer to create a polished trailer. This can add a level of professionalism that may attract more viewers.
    - **Examples**: Check out my YouTube channel for examples of book trailers I've hired professionals to create for my books "Clifton Chase and the Arrow of Light" and "The Toilet Papers: Places to Go While You Go." Additionally, watch the official movie trailer for "Just Jake," my first sold screenplay!

Book Giveaways

Generating buzz and attracting readers is a nonstop process. No matter how far up the ladder you climb, you will always need to generate buzz, attract new readers, and retain current customers. If this wasn't the case, McDonalds would stop advertising, right? Everyone knows who they are what they do, yet they still advertise, network with pop culture brands, and produce new products for their current and new customer base. You are no different.

Your book is a product. If you don't get it in front of buyers, then it won't sell. While I'm not a fan of giving away my blood, sweat, and tears, I know it's necessary at times. Here's my thoughts on book giveaways:

> 1. **Online Giveaways**: Platforms like Rafflecopter are popular for organizing book giveaways, but you can also keep everything on your website using widgets.
> 2. **Perma-Free Strategy**: Some authors make the first book in a series permanently free to funnel readers into their stories and encourage them to buy subsequent books.

Merchandise

Fans love merch! You can create brand loyalty and additional revenue streams with t-shirts, stuffed animals, customized pens, or whatever way you want to add value to your customer's experience. You can create custom gear several ways:

> 1. **On-Demand Services**: Sites like Teespring or Redbubble allow you to upload your logo or branding, handle production, and distribution on your behalf. This can be a cost-effective way

to offer merchandise without significant upfront investment.
2. **DIY Merch**: Alternatively, you can create your own merchandise to sell on your site, use as giveaways, or reward your true fans. This allows for control over quality and branding.

Sell Sheets or One Sheets

Sell sheets and one sheets are both effective tools for novelists and screenwriters:

1. **Content**: A sell sheet typically includes a logline, character descriptions, a brief synopsis, and availability information for your book or film.
2. **Design**: Use lots of images and colors to make your sell sheet visually appealing. If you need help, don't hesitate to reach out for guidance on creating effective sell sheets.

Business Essentials

It might go without saying, but you will need to invest in professional tools for building your writer brand:

1. **Business Cards, Bookmarks, Thank You Cards, and Stickers**: These items help establish your professional presence and keep you in the minds of potential readers and collaborators. On my bookmarks, I include a

CTA (Call to Action): Bring Jaimie to your school or convention. Every piece of your business is part of your marketing strategy.

2. **Branding**: Develop a cohesive brand with company colors, a logo, and a tagline that captures your essence and niche in the marketplace.

- **Example**: My brand colors are #ff1616 and #1ed5c3, my logo is my name in a fun font, and my tagline is "Stories with a Magic Touch in books, TV, and film."

Activity:

Take some time to define your brand colors, logo, and tagline. Think about what makes your work unique and how you want to be perceived in the marketplace.

Conclusion

Selling your creative work is an essential part of being a successful author or filmmaker. By leveraging tools like trailers, giveaways, merchandise, sell sheets, and business essentials, you can effectively promote your work and build a loyal audience. Remember, you are not just an artist; you are a business. Embrace these tools to turn your creativity into commerce and achieve the success you deserve.

Eight
Harnessing the Power of Social Media

In today's digital age, social media is a powerful tool for authors and filmmakers to connect with their audience, promote their work, and build their brand. However, trying to be active on every social media platform can be overwhelming and counterproductive. Instead, focus on one or two platforms where you can engage effectively.

This chapter will help you understand the pros and cons of various social media sites, guide you on setting up business pages, and explain the benefits of using analytics and ads. We'll also cover the Meta App, the importance of hashtags, and provide an overview of how to make the most out of each platform.

Choosing Your Social Media Platforms

Time is finite. Social Media isn't. There seems to be new ones popping up all the time requiring us to learn, master, and understand these platforms. It's dizzying. You could spend every hour of your day on social media and for what? What is your ROI? Do you even know?

Find one or two social sites to champion, rather than spreading yourself too thin across all platforms. If you understand how they all work, you'll be able to customize your content to the users and find your fans. Here's the tops in the industry and some of my faves:

1. **Facebook**
    - **Pros**: Wide reach, extensive ad options, robust analytics, ability to create business pages, groups, and events.
    - **Cons**: Organic reach can be limited, more competition for attention.
    - **Audience**: Broad, with a significant number of users aged 25-55.
2. **Instagram**
    - **Pros**: Visually oriented, strong engagement, features like Stories and Reels, excellent for branding.
    - **Cons**: Requires consistent, high-quality visual content.
    - **Audience**: Younger demographic, primarily 18-34.

3. **TikTok**
   - **Pros**: Rapid growth, high engagement, great for short-form video content.
   - **Cons**: Time-consuming to create content, fast-paced nature can be challenging to keep up with.
   - **Audience**: Very young, primarily 16-24.
4. **LinkedIn**
   - **Pros**: Professional network, excellent for B2B connections, thought leadership, and industry insights.
   - **Cons**: Less casual interaction, more formal content required.
   - **Audience**: Professionals, aged 25-54.
5. **Pinterest**
   - **Pros**: Doubles as a search engine, great for visual content and driving website traffic, long content lifespan.
   - **Cons**: Requires visually appealing content, less social interaction.
   - **Audience**: Predominantly female, aged 18-45.
6. **YouTube**
   - **Pros**: Video-centric, strong search engine capabilities, long content lifespan, potential for monetization.
   - **Cons**: High production effort, requires consistent content.

- Audience: Broad, with significant engagement from all age groups.
7. **Goodreads**
    - **Pros**: Focused on readers and book lovers, great for book recommendations and reviews.
    - **Cons**: Limited to book-related content, less dynamic interaction.
    - **Audience**: Book enthusiasts of all ages.

Creating a Separate Business Page

Setting up a separate business page for your author or filmmaker persona has several benefits:

- **Professionalism**: Keeps your personal and professional lives separate.
- **Analytics**: Access to detailed insights and analytics on engagement, reach, and audience demographics.
- **Ads**: Ability to run targeted ad campaigns to reach your specific audience.

Meta App for Facebook and Instagram

The Meta App allows you to connect your Facebook and Instagram business accounts on one platform. This eliminates distractions from personal feeds and helps you manage your professional presence more efficiently. You can schedule posts, respond to messages, and monitor analytics from a single interface.

Using Pinterest and YouTube as Search Engines

Both Pinterest and YouTube function as powerful search engines. Users often search for specific content, making these platforms excellent for discoverability:

- **Pinterest**: Optimize your pins with relevant keywords and hashtags to drive traffic to your website or book listings. Create boards for each book or film and fill it with pins of your dream cast, locations, relevant history or songs that would be on the soundtrack.
- **YouTube**: Use descriptive titles, tags, and video descriptions to make your content easily searchable. Use shorts to grow your brand and film your events for uploading. AI sites like Opus Clip making this process seamless!

Understanding Hashtags

Hashtags categorize content and make it discoverable to a broader audience. Here's how to use them effectively:

- **Popular Hashtags**: Use trending hashtags relevant to your content to increase visibility. Be creative! You're a writer, so find current events or viral content that runs through your story and use it. Remember I used "wolves" as my word to hit Amazon #1.

- **Branded Hashtags**: Create unique hashtags to build your brand and encourage community engagement.
  - **Example**: I use #winsfortheweek to encourage creatives to share their small weekly wins. I have #thewriteengle and #engleverse for my brand recognition.

Personal Faves

I was on 6 or 7 social media sites. I found I was posting the same information to all of them because it was quicker and easier that way. I began to notice the people I followed were doing the same thing. I felt obligated to like their post on Insta because I want the analytics to see it's a good post. Then, I'd see the same post on Facebook, and feel the same obligation. I was spending so much time posting my own content and liking everyone else's on all 6 or 7 platforms!

I decided I needed a break and took the second quarter of 2024 off everything but LinkedIn, YouTube, and Goodreads. I can't tell you how refreshed I felt. I reached my annual reading goal by April!

Now, don't get me wrong. It took me a few weeks to not constantly pick up my phone to check how my posts were doing or scrolling through Insta to see what

I'd missed. And you know what wasn't missed? Me! I didn't hear a peep from anyone until around 8 weeks off the sites and then someone texted me, "Hey, are you off Facebook?" All those posts I had curated and spent hours building and posting weren't missed. And all the time I'd wasted!

I'm not saying get off social media. Not at all! I am saying, be strategic and true to you, find where your fans are, and only post what matters to you. While I go in and out of Instagram and Facebook, I primarily use LinkedIn, YouTube, and Goodreads to connect with my audience:

- **LinkedIn**: For professional networking and sharing industry insights.
- **YouTube**: To showcase book and movie trailers, interviews, and other education video content. Shorts are great for entertaining and to tease a longer video.
- **Goodreads**: To engage with readers and gather reviews, do giveaways, and track my own reading. If someone reviews my books, as a Goodreads Author, I can like and comment on those reviews.

Conclusion

Social media is an essential tool for building your brand and connecting with your audience. By focusing on one or two platforms, creating a separate business page, and utilizing tools like the Meta App, you can manage your online presence effectively. In the next chapter, we will take a deep dive into LinkedIn and Goodreads, exploring how to leverage these platforms for maximum impact.

Nine
Mastering LinkedIn and Goodreads for Writers

In this chapter, we'll explore the powerful social media platforms LinkedIn and Goodreads. Both offer unique opportunities for writers to connect, promote, and grow their audience. We'll start with a deep dive into LinkedIn and then move on to Goodreads.

LinkedIn: A Professional Network for Writers

1. Optimizing Your LinkedIn Profile

Headline and Summary:

- **Headline**: Use a compelling headline that highlights your role as a writer, such as "Award-Winning Author & Screenwriter" or "Fantasy Novelist & Storytelling Expert."

- **Summary**: Craft a concise summary that showcases your writing journey, key accomplishments, and what you're currently working on. Include links to your books, films, awards, and projects.

Experience and Accomplishments:

- **Experience**: List your writing roles, including freelance projects, book publications, screenplay credits, and relevant work experience.
- **Accomplishments**: Highlight your awards, publications, speaking engagements, and significant milestones in your career.

Featured Section:

- Use the featured section to showcase available manuscripts or screenplays, book trailers, and other key projects. This section allows you to pin important content at the top of your profile.

2. Connecting with Professionals

Networking Opportunities:

- LinkedIn is a hub for connecting with other writers, producers, agents, and fans. Use the platform to network with professionals who can help advance your career.

- **Caveat** – When you connect, use the direct message feature and say, "Thanks for connecting!" Then, wait. Do not pitch or send links or ask questions unless they start that conversation. If they reply in kind, move on. If they reply with questions or comments, get to know them. Once you've established a business conversation, you can bring up your business.

Posting Content:

- Post updates with pictures, words, or videos to engage your network. Share writing updates, event images, blog posts, links to new YouTube videos, contract signings, new books or scripts, and in-person or virtual events.

Blogging and Newsletters:

- Utilize LinkedIn's blogging and newsletter features to build a following and convert those followers into fans. Share insights on your writing process, industry trends, and personal stories.

3. Leveraging LinkedIn Features

Verification and Live:

- Get verified to increase your credibility. Use LinkedIn Live to host events, share book launches, or conduct Q&A sessions.

Groups and Events:

- Create or join groups related to your genre or writing interests. Add speaking gigs or book signings as events on your page and invite others to attend.

Direct Messages (DM):

- Many opportunities can arise from direct messages. Producers, clients, agents, and co-writers may reach out to you based on your self-promotion efforts.

4. Personal Usage Example

I use LinkedIn to find producers, clients, and network with other screenwriters. It serves as my events hub and self-promotion platform. Daily, I post writing updates, event images, blog posts, YouTube links, contract signings, new projects, and updates on my publications and awards. Many producers I work with have reached out via LinkedIn DMs due to my self-promotion. I've also connected with agents and co-writers on this incredible site.

Goodreads: The Social Network for Readers

1. What is Goodreads?

Goodreads is like Facebook for voracious readers. It's a platform where readers and authors can connect, share book recommendations, and engage with each other's reading habits.

2. How Goodreads Works

Groups and Reviewers:

> • Find or create groups related to your genre or interests. Network with other readers and writers, and find reviewers who can help boost your book's visibility.

Posts and Updates:

> • Share updates about your writing process, book releases, and events. Connect your website blog to your Goodreads author account for seamless content sharing.
> • Share your books to the general feed any time. Goodreads will share your post with your book cover and title and you do nothing! It's amazing.
> • Take advantage of the feed and like or comment on your friends' updates. Likewise,

read reviews on your books from readers and feel free to like and thank them for all 4- and 5-star reviews. Do nothing for any reviews 3 and under.

Author Account:

- Create an author account to manage your book listings, engage with readers, and run giveaways for new releases.

3. Leveraging Goodreads Features

Giveaways and Ads:

- Offer giveaways to generate buzz for new releases. Goodreads requires entrants to add your book to their To-Be-Read (TBR) shelf, increasing visibility. You can also create ads to reach a wider audience.
- Once your book goes live, Goodreads will automatically email everyone who has added your book to their TBR shelf to let them know your book is newly released, with a link to Amazon. For FREE! This is a great feature so take advantage.
- There are two paid giveaways to choose from, as of the writing of this book. One is $99-$119. The other is $399-$599 and from experience, there isn't much of a difference between them. If you can afford the premium, do that, but if not, you're not missing out on much.

Reviews and Comments:

> • Share reviews of books you've enjoyed, including your own. Thank reviewers for their feedback and answer reader questions.

Soliciting Reviews:

> • Reach out to readers and reviewers to solicit reviews for your books. Share books with others to build your presence on the platform.

4. Utilizing the General Update Button

The general update button on Goodreads allows you to share news unrelated to physical books, such as upcoming events or new courses. This is the only place where you can add a hyperlink, making it a valuable tool for driving traffic. You can also post a picture but you have to use html code, so that is something you will have to search for on the web.

5. Pre-Publication Book Listings

One of Goodreads' coolest features is the ability to add a book even if it's just an idea. Add a generic or blank book cover, the title or genre, a projected publication date, and a brief summary or logline. Once it's uploaded, it will be given a permalink which you can share with fans while you're writing and editing your book. It's a placeholder, where you can send fans to add it to their TBR shelf. Encourage them in social posts via your CTA. When the book releases, Goodreads will notify them, providing purchase links to Amazon for free.

6. Running Giveaways

When you run a giveaway on Goodreads, entrants must add your book to their TBR shelf. After the contest ends and winners receive their free copies, Goodreads will keep the entrant list until you publish the book. Upon release, they send an email to non-winners, encouraging them to buy your book on Amazon, significantly boosting your book's visibility and sales. For free.

Conclusion

Both LinkedIn and Goodreads offer unique opportunities for writers to connect, promote, and grow their audience. By leveraging the features and networks available on these platforms, you can enhance your visibility and engage with your readers and industry professionals more effectively. I encourage you to find me on LinkedIn and Goodreads, connect with me, let me know in a DM that you read this book, and please review it on Goodreads!

Stay tuned for the next chapter, where we will dive into your newsletter.

Ten
Building Your Fanbase with a Newsletter

Owning your audience is crucial in today's digital age. If you rely solely on social media platforms to connect with your fans, you don't truly own that relationship—the platform does. Remember Twitter? The powerhouse brand is now deemed 'X' and many of the creators who had tens of hundreds of thousands of fans lost them. Or what if you deactivate or delete your account? Worse, what if someone hacks your Insta and pretends to be you? Think about all those "followers" you have no way of reaching.

Building your email list through a website and newsletter ensures you have direct contact with your audience, allowing you to engage with them on your terms. This chapter explores the importance of having a website, the benefits of an onsite newsletter, and how to effectively build and manage your email list.

The Importance of a Website

A website is your digital home base, a central hub where fans can learn about you, your work, and how to connect with you. It allows you to control your content, brand, and interactions without the constraints of social media algorithms or platform policies. Here are key benefits:

1. **Ownership of Content and Audience:** Unlike social media, your website is a space you fully control. This ensures that your content remains accessible regardless of changes to social media platforms.
2. **Centralized Information:** A well-organized website provides all the necessary information about your books, films, projects, and events in one place.
3. **Professional Presence:** A dedicated website enhances your professional image and credibility.

Building and Managing Your Email List

Some people say email is dead. Others swear by it. You'll have to decide for yourself. For me, my email list is my most important marketing asset. I spend more time on my list than on any other aspect of customer or client engagement. Why build an email list?

1. **Direct Contact**: Emails provide a direct line of communication with your audience, free from social media algorithms.
2. **Engagement and Loyalty**: Regular newsletters help maintain engagement and build loyalty among your fans.
3. **Marketing and Sales**: Email marketing is one of the most effective ways to promote your work, run promotions, and drive sales.

Tools for Building Your CRM

Two popular email marketing platforms are MailChimp and Constant Contact. Here's an overview:

MailChimp:

- **Pros**: User-friendly interface, free tier for small lists, robust analytics, integration with various platforms, and customizable templates.
- **Cons**: Higher pricing tiers can be expensive as your list grows, and limited customer support on lower tiers.
- **Pricing**: Free for up to 2,000 contacts, with paid plans starting at $10/month.

Constant Contact:

- **Pros**: Excellent customer support, easy-to-use drag-and-drop editor, extensive templates, and event management tools.
- **Cons**: More expensive than MailChimp, fewer integrations.
- **Pricing**: Plans start at $20/month.

Using Links and Popups

1. **Bitly**: Use Bitly to create trackable links that help you see where your subscribers are coming from.
2. **Subscription Links and Popups**: Invite people to subscribe via a link to a form or use popups on your website. You can also add subscribers manually from in-person events or giveaways.

Creating Segmented Lists

Segment your audience to tailor your communication effectively:

- **Reader Path**: For fans of your books.
- **Viewer Path**: For those interested in your films.
- **Educator Path**: For teachers and educators.
- **Student Path**: For aspiring writers.

Personal Example: My Website Strategy

I choose to utilize the widgets offered on my website host, WordPress, to keep everything streamlined. My fans can read a blog post, join my newsletter, follow my student path, visit my shop, and use the contact form—all on one site. This approach simplifies the process for my audience and ensures I maintain direct contact through the emails I collect.

There are so many widgets, too. I can fundraise for a new comic book. I can use forms to collect information or send invoices. I can even connect to my books on Amazon and offer my visitors a list of my titles, a chance to sample the first few pages, and a clickable link to Amazon to purchase the book, all by using a widget that requires the book link. I don't do anything technical. It's all built into the widget.

Crafting Your Newsletter

Sending a monthly newsletter is a great way to keep your audience engaged. You can personalize the opening paragraph to talk about who you are, what's happening in your personal life, and ask questions of your readers. You can include links to your shop, new courses, and merch. Your newsletter is the golden ticket to your success! Here is a template for your newsletter:

1. **Subject Header**: Include the month and your name (e.g., "June Updates from [Your Name]").

2. **Subheader**: Pose a question to intrigue readers (e.g., "What's new in the world of [Your Name]?").
3. **Monthly Updates**: Share updates on your writing, speaking engagements, client work, and movie business.
4. **Links**: Include links to your courses, store, and other relevant content.
5. **Recommendations**: Share what you're listening to on podcasts, along with an Amazon Affiliate link to the book you're currently reading.
6. **Review Reminder**: Encourage readers to review your books and films, with links to Amazon, Goodreads, and BookBub.
7. **Segmentation Buttons**: Add buttons to segment your audience into readers, writers, viewers, etc.
8. **Giveaways**: Highlight any ongoing giveaways.
9. **Subscriber-Only Content**: Provide a link to a secret website page with exclusive content like movie posters, scores, short stories, and recipes.
10. **Engagement Opportunities**: Include a button to Google Forms for fans to sign up as ARC readers, name a character, or other interactive options.

I encourage you to include a bitly link (which I'll explain later, I promise) to your newsletter sign up in every social post that doesn't have a built in CTA. What

I mean is if you aren't promoting a book, an event, or linking out to something specific, you can always add something like, "For FOMO protection, subscribe to my monthly newsletter" or "Not an Engleversian? Click to join the Engleverse today and get subscriber FIRST news!"

*Note: FOMO means "Fear of missing out." And my universe is called the Engleverse and my follower are called Engleversians. If you haven't named your brand and fans yet, I encourage you to give it some thought.

Conclusion

Building and managing an email list through your website is essential for owning your audience and maintaining direct contact. Use tools like MailChimp or Constant Contact to create and manage your lists effectively or use widgets on your website.

By streamlining your processes and keeping everything on one platform, you can enhance your engagement and conversion rates. In the next chapter, we'll dive deeper into the importance of having a website and explore all the ways to utilize it for both you and your fans.

Eleven
Enhancing Your Fanbase with a Robust Website

Building and maintaining a website is essential for writers and creatives. It's your digital home where you can connect with your audience, sell your products, and control your brand. In this chapter, we'll explore the basics of creating a website, discuss various hosting platforms, explain the importance of integrating tools and services, and delve into the myriad ways a website can help build and engage your fanbase.

Website Basics

This is a technical section. Not everyone is capable of creating and managing their own website. I totally understand. I used to be you. I spent hundreds of hours messing around with the platforms until I became proficient enough to manage my own site. You can absolutely hire someone to do it for you! They can design, enhance, maintain, and watch over your site for you. If you can't afford it or if you enjoy being at the helm, here are some website hosts and domains I work with:

1. **Choosing a Platform:**
   - **WordPress:** Highly customizable with a wide range of plugins and themes. Great for blogging and e-commerce.
   - **Wix:** User-friendly with drag-and-drop features. Ideal for beginners and small businesses.
   - **Squarespace:** Sleek designs with built-in e-commerce features. Good for creatives who want a polished look without extensive customization.
2. **Domains:** Your domain name is your website's address (e.g., www.yourname.com). Choose a domain that reflects your brand and is easy to remember. I prefer GoDaddy, but you can search for your favorite.

Integration with E-Commerce Tools

1. **WooCommerce:** A powerful plugin for WordPress that allows you to sell products online, manage inventory, and track sales.
2. **PayPal and Square:** Both offer hardware and software solutions for processing payments in-person and online, tracking inventory, and managing sales tax.

Selling and Connecting with Fans

1. **Widgets:** Widgets are tools that you can add to your website to provide additional functionality,

such as social media feeds, contact forms, and newsletter sign-ups.
   - **Example:** I use MailPoet for my newsletter, Amazon widgets for book previews, and various social media widgets to keep my site interactive and engaging.

Creating Pages for Different Audiences

1. **Press Page:** Include your expert press release, high-resolution photos, and contact information for media inquiries.
2. **Teacher and Conference Page:** List your presentation options, descriptions, and a resume of previous engagements.
3. **About Page:** Share your journey, passion, and why you write. This page is often used by teachers and event organizers to introduce you.
4. **Blog Page:** Regularly update your blog to engage with your audience and share insights into your writing process.
5. **Contact Page:** Ensure your contact form is easy to find and directs messages to your email inbox.

Merchandise and Sales Integration

1. **Merchandise Page:** Sell signed books, t-shirts, and other branded merchandise.
   - **Printful and Print Aura:** These services handle production and distribution of your merchandise. Printful also allows integration with your site for seamless transactions.

- **Etsy, TikTok, Pinterest, Instagram, Amazon, Shopify, and Facebook Shops**: Expand your sales channels by setting up shops on these platforms.

Courses and Digital Products

Offer courses and downloadable products directly from your site. This keeps your audience engaged and provides additional revenue streams.

Private and Exclusive Pages

1. **Newsletter Fan Page**: As mentioned in the previous chapter, you can create a password-protected page with exclusive content like downloadable posters, film scores, short stories, and recipes.
2. **Screenplay Offerings**: For screenwriters, have password-protected pages with scripts, treatments, and pitch decks. This ensures producers always access the latest versions.

My scripts are all housed on my website and password protected. Here's why I love this feature. Besides looking VERY professional and totally together, I have been at my son's high school football game, been texted by a producer looking for one of my scripts or decks, and literally texted them the web link and password from the bleachers. How freaking cool is that?

Calendar Integration

Connect your calendar to your website to automatically update events. This feature allows fans to see your upcoming appearances and engagements. You can use Google or iCalendar or register with a third-party widget.

Regular Updates and Maintenance

Review your website quarterly to ensure all information is current, new books or merch are added, and your brand message remains clear. Regular updates help maintain a professional and engaging site.

My Website Journey Revisited

As mentioned in the previous chapter, I use WordPress to host my website, keeping everything centralized for my fans. They can read blog posts, join my newsletter, follow my student path, visit my shop, and use the contact form—all in one place. I regularly update pages with new books, merchandise, and speaking engagements, ensuring my audience always has access to the latest information.

Conclusion

A well-maintained website is crucial for building and engaging your fanbase. By integrating various tools and features, you can create a seamless experience for your audience, from discovering your work to purchasing products and engaging with your content. In the next chapter, we'll jump into the riveting world of speaking engagements, the revenue stream you will fall in love with!

Twelve
Mastering Speaking Engagements to Expand Your Reach

Speaking engagements are a powerful way to connect with your audience, share your passion, and sell your books or scripts. Whether you're presenting at conferences, community events, libraries, schools, or conventions, each opportunity can help you grow your fanbase and establish yourself as an expert in your field.

This chapter will guide you through finding speaking engagements, preparing for them, and creating repeat customers.

Finding Speaking Engagements

Don't overthink it. You don't have to get it right; you just have to get it going! You have a unique perspective and POV that an audience is waiting for. You wrote your story because you are passionate about it. I guarantee you aren't alone. All you have to do is find your audience, practice for free, and work on your presentation. Let's begin with the first part, find your audience:

1. **Conferences:**

   - **Industry Conferences:** Look for conferences related to books, writing, film, and your specific genres or topics. Examples include literary festivals, writer's conferences, and film festivals.
   - **Community Events:** Local events such as family festivals, B2B events, and other community gatherings can be excellent venues to reach new audiences.

2. **Libraries and Schools:**

   - **Libraries:** Offer to do readings, participate in summer programs, or be part of library conventions. Libraries often welcome authors for events and book signings.
   - **Schools:** From elementary schools to colleges, schools are great places to share your writing journey and inspire students. Tailor your presentations to fit the age group and educational needs.

3. **Conventions and Guilds:**

- **Conventions**: Attend conventions related to your book or film's genre. Comic conventions, homeschool conventions, and niche interest conventions (e.g., medical, home improvement) can be unique opportunities to reach your audience.
- **Guilds**: Writer's guilds, BNI networking groups, Rotary Clubs, Chamber of Commerce organizations, and other professional groups often seek speakers for their meetings.

4. **Subject Matter Expert:**

- As discussed in the press release chapter, positioning yourself as a subject matter expert can lead to speaking engagements. Offer your expertise on relevant topics to various organizations.

Starting Small and Growing Your Confidence

If you're new to speaking, start with smaller events to build your confidence and experience. You may need to offer your services for free or even pay for your event space initially. Here's how to get started:

1. **Offer Free Talks in Exchange for a Table:**

- Reach out to conventions or conferences and propose speaking on a related topic for free in exchange for a table to sell your books. This helps you practice speaking without the pressure of paid engagements.

2. Community Events:

- Attend local events and fairs. These venues can be surprisingly effective for selling books and connecting with new fans. Think creatively about how your book's themes can tie into different types of events.

3. Libraries and Schools:

- Libraries and schools often have limited budgets, so offering free talks can open doors. Over time, as you gain experience and recognition, you can start charging for your time.

In addition, schools often have literacy related events, like Suess Day and Literacy Week, which are great times for you to talk about being a writer, regardless of your book's audience age. Also, schools often have Career Days, where members of the community come into speak about their jobs and encourage students to think outside the box of potential career fields. Writers are perfect presenters to discuss jobs like being a journalist, a novelist, and a screenwriter or as a social media strategist, technical writer, or blogger. Reach out to the schools and libraries in your area and be read to fill your calendar!

Tips for Successful Speaking Engagements

1. **Prepare Thoroughly**: Know your material well, practice your delivery, and anticipate possible questions.
2. **Engage Your Audience**: Use visuals, stories, and interactive elements to keep your audience engaged.
3. **Collect Emails**: Always bring a sign-in sheet to collect email addresses for your newsletter. This step is crucial for building your contact list.
4. **Bring Marketing Materials**: Have business cards, bookmarks, and other materials to hand out. Make it easy for people to remember you and find your work.
5. **Follow Up**: Send thank-you emails and keep in touch with event organizers and attendees. Building relationships can lead to repeat invitations and new opportunities.

Conventions and Creative Speaking Opportunities

1. **Homeschool Conventions**: Offer to speak about your book and provide educational resources, such as teacher guides.
2. **Niche Conventions**: Tailor your presentations to fit the theme of the convention. For

example, use a werewolf novel to discuss STEM science on wolves.

Guilds and Networking Groups

1. **Writer's Guilds and Professional Groups**: Many people aspire to write a book. Speaking at these events can help you connect with potential collaborators and readers.
2. **BNI, Rotary Clubs, and Chamber of Commerce**: These groups are always looking for engaging speakers. Share your writing journey and how it applies to business or personal development.

School Visits

1. **Program Offerings**: Develop presentations that are educational and entertaining. Use your books as a foundation to teach about writing, storytelling, and relevant life lessons.
2. **Pre-Visit Videos**: Introduce yourself and your books to students before the visit. This builds excitement and familiarity.
3. **Book Orders**: Send out order forms before and after your visit to maximize book sales.
4. **Follow-Up Videos**: Remind students of your visit and encourage them to read and review your books.

Creating Repeat Customers

1. **Deliver Value:** Ensure your presentations are valuable and memorable. This encourages organizers to invite you back.
2. **Build Relationships:** Stay in touch with event organizers and attendees. Personal connections can lead to future opportunities.
3. **Offer New Content:** Keep your presentations fresh and relevant. As you create new books or projects, update your offerings to reflect your latest work.

Conclusion

Speaking engagements are a powerful way to connect with your audience, build your brand, and sell your books or films. By starting small, growing your confidence, and continuously seeking new opportunities, you can become a sought-after speaker. Reach out to various venues, deliver valuable content, and always look for ways to build lasting relationships. The next chapter extends this idea into learning the art of self-promotion. Get ready!

Thirteen
The Art of Self-Promotion

Self-promotion is an essential aspect of building a successful writing career. It's not just about selling books or scripts; it's about selling yourself. People want to do business with people they know and trust. This chapter delves into the nuances of self-promotion and why it's crucial for your business.

Podcasts and YouTube interviews are excellent ways to get in front of people, share your story, and gain new followers. These platforms allow you to connect with your audience on a personal level, letting them hear your voice and see your passion. For instance, I once landed a gig writing a treatment for a Hollywood producer who first heard me on a podcast. They watched my movie "Just Jake" and decided I was the right person for their project. It was me they connected with first; my film just confirmed their decision. Remember, people want to get to know you before they decide to work with you. You can be an incredible writer, but if you're difficult to work with, it won't matter. You are not a green M&M star, so don't act like one. Even if you are, don't!

Part of your self-promotion strategy might include a book launch. While I'm not a big fan personally, I know many writers who find it beneficial. If you're looking for a professional company to help launch your book, I highly recommend RABT Book Tours. Cami Hensley, the owner, truly cares about her business and her writers. She offers book tours, review services, and virtual assistants. Mention my name for a small discount on my next purchase. Thanks in advance! ☺

Self-promotion can be challenging if you don't have anything to promote, right? Don't worry! You write fiction for a living, so write one for yourself. Make yourself desirable until you're desired. Let me say that again: make yourself desirable until you're desired. How do you do that? Share your journey. I've climbed the Hollywood ladder by doing just that.

When I was waiting for my movie contract and shooting schedule, which took almost two years, I spent that time working, learning, and writing. Each time I took an online writing course, SNAP! I took a selfie and posted it. Each time I met with my writing mentor, SNAP! I took a selfie and shared it. Every milestone, every production meeting, every agent reading my query letter, every contest win for my latest script went on my social media with an exciting caption and my branded hashtag #winsfortheweek.

That was all I did. I worked, I wrote, I submitted, and I shared. You can do the same. My self-promotion strategy brought producers to my direct messages on LinkedIn and actors to my DMs on Instagram. I took meetings with major Hollywood producers and signed contracts for the development of several of my movie and television scripts. All because they wanted to learn who I was, what I was about, and what I was passionate about. Then, they wanted to help me succeed and open doors for me to find my next step in the movie-making process. It's been an absolutely wild ride, and I'm having a blast.

You don't need to spend a dime to self-promote. Whether you choose to promote in person or online, you can network with anyone, anywhere in the world, with a little consistency, dedication, and a big smile.

Before we move on to the next chapter, I have some questions for you, the reader of my book.

- What is your purpose?
- Why are you writing your book or script?
- Who is your target audience?
- How much time do you have to commit to writing, editing, and marketing?
- How much money do you have to commit to writing, editing, and marketing?
- What are your writing goals, short-term and long-term?
- And finally, what are your goals?

- To sell more books or scripts?
- Increase your fanbase?
- Increase the number of quality reviews?
- Create a credible platform?

Answering these questions will help you figure out your self-promotion strategy. Once you nail that, you'll be ready to create multiple products for your audience through cross mediums, which we will discuss in the next chapter.

Fourteen
Exploring Cross-Medium Storytelling

Welcome to one of the most exciting chapters of "Plotting Profits." If you've made it this far, you're ready to explore the diverse and lucrative world of cross-medium storytelling. In today's commoditized world, writing a book is a significant achievement, but it's often not enough. Writing ten books might not even be enough. Screenwriting is a long and uncertain journey from idea to the big screen, and factors like the Hollywood WGA strikes can disrupt a writer's livelihood. However, if you love writing, the medium shouldn't matter. Cross-medium storytelling encourages writers to expand their skills and fanbase by utilizing various forms of storytelling. Let's dive into the myriad possibilities.

Kindle Vella: Episodic Storytelling

Kindle Vella is Amazon's platform for serialized storytelling. It allows writers to publish stories one episode at a time, engaging readers with regular updates.

How It Works:

- Writers publish episodes, and readers purchase tokens to unlock them.
- The first few episodes are free, allowing readers to sample the story before committing.

Benefits:

- **For Writers**: Regular feedback from readers, potential for steady income, and increased reader engagement.
- **For Fans**: Immediate access to new episodes, interactive features like thumbs up, and the ability to follow favorite stories.

Negative Aspects:

- **For Writers**: The need for frequent updates can be demanding, and income is dependent on consistent reader engagement.
- **For Fans**: Episodes cost tokens, which can add up, and stories might get abandoned by writers.

Audiobooks: The Growing Market

Audiobooks have seen a significant rise in popularity, offering a convenient way for people to consume stories.

Stats and Benefits:

- **Listenership**: Audiobooks are popular among commuters, multitaskers, and people with visual impairments.
- **Sales**: The audiobook market has grown consistently, often outperforming eBook and print sales in certain genres.

Creating Audiobooks:

- Hire a professional narrator or narrate your own book.
- Use platforms like ACX to produce and distribute your audiobook.

Adapting Stories Across Mediums

One of the most rewarding aspects of cross-medium storytelling is the ability to adapt your story into different formats, reaching new audiences each time.

Short Stories to Screenplays:

- Adapt a short story into a screenplay or teleplay to explore visual storytelling.

- Example: A short story can be expanded with dialogue and scenes to fit the screenplay format, reaching film and TV audiences.

Screenplays to Comics:

- Use your screenplay as the basis for a comic book or graphic novel. Comics are visual and can be a proof of concept for your script at a fraction of the cost of a sizzle reel.
- Example: Publish webcomics or self-publish through platforms like ComiXology.

Books to Film or TV:

- Adapt your novel into a screenplay for film or TV. Each medium has different storytelling rules and audience expectations.
- Example: Transform your novel's narrative into a visual script, exploring new aspects of your story.

Expanding Your Story Universe

Cross-medium storytelling also includes creating spinoffs, series, prequels, and one-shots, each in different mediums.

Spinoffs and Prequels:

- Create spinoffs focusing on side characters or specific story elements.
- Write prequels to explore the backstory of your main narrative.

Series and One-Shots:

- Continue your story in a series format, either in the same medium or different ones.
- Write one-shots to delve deeper into specific events or characters.

Non-Fiction Support Books

Create non-fiction books that complement your fiction works.

Example:

- After publishing a comic book, I created a blank comic book for kids to illustrate their own stories.
- Turn your class presentation into a comprehensive guidebook, like this book "Plotting Profits."

Creative Cross-Medium Ideas

Think outside the box and find creative ways to expand your story.

Examples:

- Turn a newspaper article from your novel into a blog post.
- Write the prophecy book mentioned in your fantasy novel as a real book for fans to read.
- Discuss your process, characters, and settings through a YouTube channel or vlog your journey

Conclusion

The opportunities for cross-medium storytelling are endless. By exploring different mediums, you can reach new audiences, expand your creative skills, and increase your income streams. Remember to align your cross-medium projects with your overall goals and fanbase, ensuring that each new venture supports and enhances your original work. For more inspiration and guidance, check out the book *You're Gonna Need a Bigger Story* by Houston Howard. It's mind blowing.

Next, we will discuss the importance of connecting with your audience through various channels, ensuring your stories reach as many people as possible and create lasting impact.

Fifteen
Final Tips and Tricks for Expanding Your Writing Business

As we wrap up "Plotting Profits," I want to leave you with some final tips and tools to help you continue building your writing career and expanding your income streams. These resources will enhance your online presence, streamline your promotional efforts, and open up new revenue opportunities. Let's dive into these valuable tools and tips.

WebStatsDomain.org

WebStatsDomain.org is a useful tool for analyzing your website's performance. It provides detailed information about your site's traffic, global ranking, and other important metrics. Use it to:

- **Track Visitor Data**: Understand where your visitors are coming from and which pages they visit most.
- **Analyze Competitors**: Compare your site with competitors to identify areas for improvement.
- **Improve SEO**: Use the insights to optimize your website for better search engine rankings.

Opus Clip

Opus Clip is a powerful tool for creating professional-quality video clips from your longer video content, helping you engage your audience effectively.

- **Repurpose Content**: Easily create engaging clips from existing videos to maximize content use.
- **Boost Engagement**: Tailor clips for social media to increase likes, shares, and comments.
- **Drive Traffic**: Use clips to direct viewers to your full-length content and products.

Canva

Canva is a versatile graphic design tool that's perfect for creating eye-catching visuals for your promotions.

- **Create Book Covers**: Design professional-quality book covers for self-publishing.
- **Social Media Graphics**: Make engaging posts, banners, and stories for social media.

- **Marketing Materials**: Design flyers, posters, and promotional materials for your events.

BookBrush

BookBrush is a design tool specifically tailored for authors.

- **3D Book Covers**: Create stunning 3D mockups of your book covers for marketing.
- **Promotional Images**: Design eye-catching promotional images for ads, social media, and your website.
- **Video Creators**: Make book trailers and promotional videos easily.

Google My Business

Google My Business helps you manage your online presence across Google, including search and maps.

- **Local SEO**: Improve your visibility in local searches, making it easier for local readers to find you.
- **Customer Engagement**: Post updates, respond to reviews, and share important information about your business.
- **Insights**: Access analytics to see how customers interact with your business profile.

Google Alerts

Google Alerts is a free tool that notifies you whenever your specified keywords appear online.

- **Monitor Mentions**: Keep track of mentions of your name, book titles, or topics of interest.
- **Stay Updated**: Receive alerts about industry news, trends, and relevant content.
- **Competitive Analysis**: Monitor competitors and see what they're up to.

Beacons and Linktree

Beacons and Linktree are tools that help you create a single link with multiple destinations, perfect for social media bios.

- **Centralized Links**: Combine all your important links (website, social media, books, etc.) into one.
- **Customizable**: Tailor the appearance and organization to match your branding.
- **Analytics**: Track clicks and interactions to understand what your audience engages with most.

Bit.ly

Bit.ly is a URL shortening service that offers more than just short links.

- **Trackable Links:** Monitor the performance of your links, including clicks and engagement.
- **Branded Links:** Create custom short links that reinforce your brand.
- **Analytics:** Gain insights into your audience's behavior and preferences.

Amazon Affiliate Program

The Amazon Affiliate program is a fantastic way to earn additional income by promoting products, including books and other items.

- **Sign Up:** Join the Amazon Associates program to start earning commissions.
- **Create Links:** Generate affiliate links for any product on Amazon, including books you've read and your own books.
- **Promote:** Share these links on your website, blog, social media, and newsletters.
- **Earn Commissions:** Earn a percentage of the sales made through your affiliate links.

Benefits:

- **Passive Income:** Earn money every time someone makes a purchase through your link.
- **Wide Range of Products:** Promote not just books, but any product on Amazon.
- **Trustworthy Platform:** Leverage Amazon's reputation to boost your credibility.

Other Affiliate Opportunities

Expand your affiliate marketing efforts with other programs:

- **Audible:** Promote audiobooks and earn commissions on memberships and audiobook sales.
- **ShareASale:** Join a network of various affiliate programs across different industries.
- **Brand Partnerships:** Reach out to companies you love and use, such as Happy Planner, Final Draft, Microsoft Word, and reMarkable, to explore affiliate or sponsorship opportunities.

Benefits:

- **Diversified Income:** Multiple streams of income from different affiliate programs.
- **Aligned Partnerships:** Promote products you genuinely use and believe in, adding authenticity to your recommendations.

Conclusion

Self-promotion and diversifying your income streams are essential strategies for a successful writing career. By leveraging tools like WebStatsDomain.org, Opus Clip, Canva, BookBrush, Google My Business, Google Alerts, Beacons, Linktree, and Bit.ly, you can enhance your online presence and track your progress effectively. Additionally, tapping into affiliate programs like Amazon Associates, Audible, and ShareASale, and partnering with brands you trust, can create new revenue opportunities.

Remember, your journey as a writer is not just about creating great content but also about smartly promoting it and exploring every available avenue to share your passion with the world.

Thank you for joining me on this journey, and I hope "Plotting Profits" has provided you with the insights and tools needed to build a successful, diverse, and fulfilling writing career. Keep writing, keep promoting, and keep growing your brand.

Parting Thoughts

Thank you for reading *Plotting Profits*. I am thrilled for you as you embark on your journey to build a successful book and/or screenwriting business. Remember, achieving success as a writer involves understanding the different Writer Types we discussed in the first chapter.

Now that you know what it takes to succeed, ask yourself again: Which Writer are you or what kind of writer are you? I'd love for you to share your answer with me. Visit my website or DM me on Linkedin (www.JaimieEngle.com/contact or www.Linkedin.com/in/jaimieenglewrites)

Summary of Main Chapter Points:

- **Chapter 1: Understanding Writer Types**: Identifying your strengths and areas for growth.
- **Chapter 2: Discovering Your "Why"**: Finding your mission and purpose as a writer.
- **Chapter 3: Press Kits**: Crafting and utilizing effective press kits.

- **Chapter 4: Book Reviews**: The importance of reviews and how to get them.
- **Chapter 5: Movie Reviews**: Where to find and how to use them.
- **Chapter 6: Book Awards**: Submitting your work for awards and using accolades in marketing.
- **Chapter 7: Selling Tools**: Various tools and strategies for selling your books and scripts.
- **Chapter 8: Social Media**: Leveraging social media platforms to connect with your audience.
- **Chapter 9: LinkedIn and Goodreads**: Deep dive into these platforms for professional networking and reader engagement.
- **Chapter 10: Newsletter**: Building your fanbase with a newsletter.
- **Chapter 11: Website**: Enhancing your fanbase with a robust website.
- **Chapter 12: Speaking Engagements**: Finding and succeeding in speaking opportunities.
- **Chapter 13: Self-Promotion**: Effective strategies for promoting yourself and your work.
- **Chapter 14: Cross-Medium Storytelling**: Expanding your storytelling across various mediums.
- **Chapter 15: Final Tips and Tricks**: Tools and resources to enhance your writing business.

Your Central Intention: Creating a Business Plan

It's essential to define your central intention and create a business plan to guide your journey. Take some time to answer these questions:

1. What do you most value?
2. What kind of life do you want to live?
3. What do you wish to become?
4. What do you wish your day-to-day life to look like?
5. What would you like to be doing in 6 months, 1 year, 2 years?
6. How much money will you need to live in your current or desired lifestyle and by when?
7. Do you have enough good ideas and work ethic to be effective?
8. Are there enough customers to support your business?

After answering these questions, consider: **How will writing books or screenplays help you achieve this central intention?**

Parting Encouragement and Nuggets of Truth

Remember, you are a small business owner. Whether you are an author, agent, and publisher, or a writer, developer, and producer, your book or script is another product in the marketplace. Your job is to find and sell to your target market. Your job is to keep records and create duplicable systems. You are not just an artist; you are an ENTREPRENEUR. Most small businesses fail within the first year, so how are you going to overcome this challenge?

Encouragement:

- **Stay Persistent**: The road to success is long and challenging, but persistence pays off.
- **Be Adaptable**: The industry and market trends can change. Stay flexible and adapt your strategies.
- **Continue Learning**: Invest in your growth by learning new skills and improving your craft.
- **Network**: Build relationships with other writers, industry professionals, and your audience.

Thank you again for embarking on this journey with me. I wish you all the best in your writing endeavors and look forward to seeing your success. Remember, the power to achieve your dreams lies within you. Keep writing, keep promoting, and keep growing.

Don't hesitate to reach out with questions and comments or to discuss my services to help you succeed! And check out the *Plotting Profits* workbook for more actionable thought-provoking ideas.

Contact me at www.JaimieEngle.com/contact and let's take your business to the next level. Remember, the world needs your words and your voice matters.

Till the next book…

About The Author

Jaimie Engle is an award-winning writer of stories with a magic touch in film, tv and books across genres. Several of her adapted short stories and original scripts are in development with major producers and studios. She wrote the feature film JUST JAKE produced by TrueBrand Entertainment and distributed through UpTV Network (2023) and the novel adaptation published through Vinspire Publishing (2023). Besides writing, Jaimie bakes grain free, attends theater to watch her firstborn act, and cheers her youngest during Friday Night Lights with her husband.

Fun fact? Jaimie was a Hooker on *Law and Order.*